Rhinoceroses

By Stephanie Warren Drimmer

Nature's CHILDREN™

Children's Press®

An Imprint of Scholastic Inc.

Content Consultant
Adam Felts
Curator, Asia Quest and Heart of Africa
Columbus Zoo and Aquarium

Library of Congress Cataloging-in-Publication Data
Names: Drimmer, Stephanie Warren, author.
Title: Rhinoceroses/by Stephanie Warren Drimmer.
Other titles: Nature's children (New York, N.Y.)
Description: New York, NY: Children's Press, an imprint of Scholastic Inc., 2018. |
Series: Nature's children | Includes index.
Identifiers: LCCN 2017035460| ISBN 9780531234785 (library binding) | ISBN 9780531245088 (pbk.)
Subjects: LCSH: Rhinoceroses—Juvenile literature. | Endangered species—Juvenile literature.
Classification: LCC QL737.U63 D75 2018 | DDC 599.66/8—dc23
LC record available at https://lccn.loc.gov/2017035460

Design by Anna Tunick Tabachnik

Creative Direction: Judith Christ-Lafond for Scholastic

Produced by Spooky Cheetah Press

Printed in North Mankato, MN, USA   113

SCHOLASTIC, CHILDREN'S PRESS, NATURE'S CHILDREN™, and associated logos
are trademarks and/or registered trademarks of Scholastic Inc.

1 2 3 4 5 6 7 8 9 10 R 27 26 25 24 23 22 21 20 19 18

Scholastic Inc., 557 Broadway, New York, NY 10012.

Photos ©: cover: Kevin Delaney/National Geographic Creative; 1: Jeremy Cozannet/Alamy Images; 4 leaf silo and throughout:
stockgraphicdesigns.com; 5 child silo: All-Silhouettes.com; 5 bottom: Richard Du Toit/Minden Pictures; 6 rhino silo and
throughout: Miceking/Shutterstock; 7: Binty/iStockphoto; 8 bottom center right: StockPhotosArt - Animals/Alamy Images;
8 bottom right: Joel Sartore/Getty Images; 8 background-9: Alain Compost/Biosphoto; 8 bottom center left: Suzi Eszterhas/
Minden Pictures; 8 bottom left: Gary Ombler/Getty Images; 11: Gary Ombler/Getty Images; 12-13: Peter Delaney/imageBROKER/
age fotostock; 15: Tui De Roy/Minden Pictures; 16-17: Benedikt Saxler/Shutterstock; 18-19: Cyril Ruoso/Minden Pictures; 20-21:
Tony Heald/NPL/Minden Pictures; 23: M. Harvey/Abpl/age fotostock; 25: Theo_Theron/iStockphoto; 26-27: ZSSD/Minden
Pictures; 28-29: Patrick Kientz/Biosphoto/Minden Pictures; 30: Mark Newman/FLPA/Media Bakery; 33: Antoine Antoniol/
Bloomberg/Getty Images; 34-35: aleks1949/Getty Images; 37 top left: Callipso/iStockphoto; 37 top right: IanRedding/Shutterstock;
37 bottom left: Elaine Kasmer; 37 bottom right: Shattil and Rozinski/NPL/Minden Pictures; 39: Jim Brandenburg/Minden Pictures;
40: Pete Oxford/Minden Pictures; 42 center left: gualtiero boffi/Shutterstock; 42 left: Joel Sartore/Getty Images; 42 right: Joel
Sartore/Getty Images; 42 center right: GlobalP/iStockphoto; 43 bottom left: JackF/iStockphoto; 43 bottom right: Alta Oosthuizen/
Shutterstock; 43 top left: GlobalP/iStockphoto; 43 top right: Panther Media GmbH/Alamy Images.

Maps by Jim McMahon.

Table of Contents

Fact File: Rhinoceroses

World Distribution

Eastern and southern Africa; northern India and southern Nepal; Malaysia and Indonesia

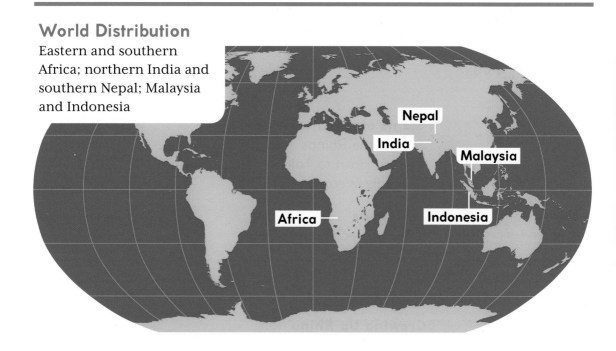

Nepal

India

Malaysia

Africa

Indonesia

Population Status

From vulnerable to critically endangered, depending on species

Habitats

Grasslands and floodplains in Africa; swamps and rain forests in Asia

Habits

Spend majority of time grazing, browsing, and wallowing in mud puddles and pools

Diet

Grasses, leaves, and shrubs

Distinctive Features

Thick, loose skin; one or two horns; massive body with sturdy legs that end in three-toed feet; amount of body hair varies by species

Fast Fact
The name rhinoceros means "nose horn."

Average Height

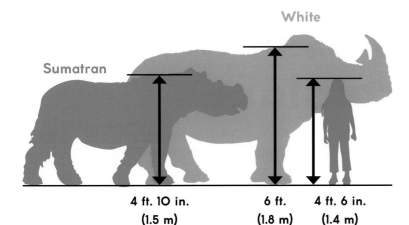

White

Sumatran

| 4 ft. 10 in. (1.5 m) | 6 ft. (1.8 m) | 4 ft. 6 in. (1.4 m) |

Rhinoceroses (at shoulder)   **Human (age 10)**

Taxonomy

CLASS
Mammalia (mammals)

ORDER
Perissodactyla (rhinoceroses, horses, and tapirs)

FAMILY
Rhinocerotidae (rhinoceroses)

GENUS
Ceratotherium, Diceros, Dicerorhinus, Rhinoceros

SPECIES
- *Ceratotherium simum* (white rhinoceros)
- *Diceros bicornis* (black rhinoceros)
- *Rhinoceros unicornis* (Indian rhinoceros)
- *Rhinoceros sondaicus* (Javan rhinoceros)
- *Dicerorhinus sumatrensis* (Sumatran rhinoceros)

◀ White rhinos can eat plants that are toxic to other animals.

CHAPTER 1

Giants of the Grasslands

It's early morning on the savanna.
Birds sing. Monkeys chatter in the treetops. Lions yawn
and stretch. The golden grasses sway as something moves
through them—something big. It's a black rhinoceros, one
of the largest land animals on Earth.

The rhino sniffs the air, raising her huge horn to the
sky. She's checking for signs of danger. Only after deciding
the grassland is safe will she step out into the open.
The reason for her caution becomes clear. Behind her,
a small baby rhino wobbles forward on shaky legs.

Rhinos are big, strong mammals that live in Africa and
southern Asia. They and their ancestors have walked the
Earth for millions of years. But now rhinos are at risk as
humans move onto their land and kill them for their horns.

▶ Black rhinos are
famous for their
short tempers!

Javan

white

black

Indian

Sumatran

8

Meet the Rhinos

There are five **species** of rhinoceros. The biggest of them all, a full-grown male white rhino, can weigh as much as 5,500 pounds (2,494.8 kilograms). Only African and Asian elephants are bigger.

White rhinos and black rhinos live in Africa. Despite their names, both are gray in color. The difference between the two is not color but the shape of their mouths. The white rhino has a flat, wide mouth. The black rhino has a pointed top lip.

Indian rhinos live in India and Nepal. They're nearly as large as white rhinos. They weigh about 4,840 lb. (2,195.4 kg) and stand nearly 6 feet (1.8 meters) tall.

The Sumatran rhino is covered in a shaggy coat. It's the only rhino with a significant amount of hair. This species is critically **endangered**: there are fewer than 100 animals left in the wild. They all live on the island of Sumatra.

Scientists don't know very much about Javan rhinos. They used to live in many tropical **habitats**. But today there is only one small **population** left.

◀ Scientists think there are fewer than 50 Javan rhinos left on Earth.

From Horn to Tail

Rhinos have big horns and heavy bodies. Their legs are like tree trunks. They are strong and powerful—and they look a little scary! But rhinos are mostly peaceful animals.

These large animals live in hot parts of the world. Their skin is layered with fat that helps keep them cool during the heat of the day. Even though a rhino's skin looks thick and tough, it's actually quite sensitive. It can get sunburned, just like our skin.

Rhinos have ears that swivel independently of each other to pick up even the softest sounds. These animals have to rely on their exceptional hearing and sense of smell because their eyesight is poor.

These massive **herbivores** spend most of their time munching on plants. Their bodies are built for this task. Short legs and a low-hanging head help them reach plants on the ground. They use their horns to break branches and dig up roots to find food.

Fast Fact
Some rhino species have one horn; others have two.

10

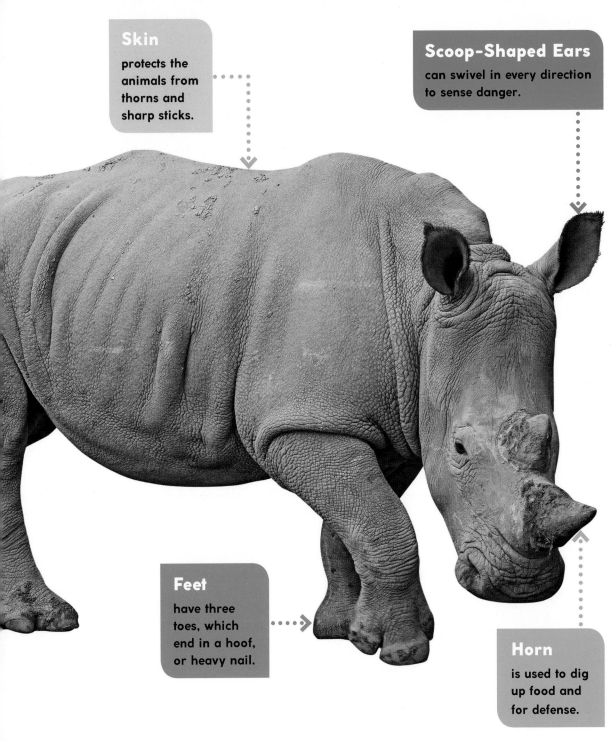

Skin
protects the animals from thorns and sharp sticks.

Scoop-Shaped Ears
can swivel in every direction to sense danger.

Feet
have three toes, which end in a hoof, or heavy nail.

Horn
is used to dig up food and for defense.

11

Deadly Weapons

The horn of a full-grown male black rhino is a fearsome sight. This deadly weapon can reach up to 4 ft. (1.2 m) long!

A rhino's horn is made of keratin. That's the same tough material that fingernails, claws, feathers, and hair are made of. Some rhinos keep their horns sharp by rubbing them against rocks and trees. If a rhino's horn breaks, a new one can regrow in its place—as long as the animal's skull isn't damaged as well.

Adult rhinos are so big and strong that they have no natural predators. But if they do feel threatened, rhinos are known to attack. A male black rhino will put his head down, point his horn out, and charge.

◀ Black rhinos can charge at 35 mph (56 kph).

CHAPTER 2

Rhino Life

It takes a lot of food to power a big body. Rhinos spend most of the morning, late afternoon, and night munching on plants. White rhinos must eat up to 120 lb. (54.4 kg) of grass every day. That's nearly equal to the weight of two 10-year-olds!

Both white and black rhinos make their homes on the African savanna. But they eat different foods. The white rhino's wide mouth is perfect for grazing on grasses. Black rhinos have a **prehensile**, or grasping, lip that's good for plucking leaves and fruit from trees and bushes.

Neither of these species has front teeth. They use their lips to tear up plants. Black rhinos sometimes stand on their hind legs to reach tasty leaves high in a tree.

▶ Rhinos (like this black rhino) can go for several days without water. They survive on the moisture found in the plants they eat.

Clever Techniques

The rhino species that live in Asia are the Indian, Javan, and Sumatran rhinos. They each have a broad mouth with a small, prehensile lip. These animals have similar eating habits to those of Africa's rhinos.

Sumatran and Javan rhinos use an unusual technique to help them reach their favorite food. They find a small tree and walk right on top of it! The rhino pushes its chest against the tree's bendy trunk and walks forward until the tree is bent over and trapped between the rhino's front legs. The fruit and leaves are now easy to reach.

◀ Indian rhinos make tunnel-like paths through the tall grasses where they live.

Keeping Cool

Rhinos never stray too far from water, like rivers, pools, and mudholes. These are good places for rhinos to get a drink when they're thirsty. They can drink up to 25 gallons (94.6 liters) of water a day! These water sources also serve as swimming holes.

Rhinos can't sweat. So they spend a lot of their time **wallowing** in muddy water to keep cool. Wallowing also helps protect their sensitive skin. A layer of mud acts like a natural sunscreen.

This pastime also helps protect rhinos from pests. That's especially important for the Asian species. Biting insects can be a big problem in their humid forest homes. Wallowing in water helps wash off bugs, and a layer of mud keeps the pests away.

▶ This rhino found a nice deep wallow. These animals sometimes roll in muddy ground to create their own mudholes.

Rhino Communication

Rhinos can't speak, but they do communicate. They use body language, sounds—and even their poop!

Rhinos **vocalize** as they near each other. They squeal, snort, and moo. A male rhino, called a bull, growls to challenge another bull to fight. Recently, scientists discovered that rhinos use **infrasonic** sounds, as well. Those are too low for humans to hear. The Sumatran rhino's call can carry 12 miles (19.3 kilometers)!

Rhinos use their bodies to communicate, too. To show affection, two rhinos might rub their sides against each other. Perked ears mean a rhino is curious. Flattened earns warn, "Stay away!" That's how a male rhino might signal to another to keep out of his **territory**.

◀ A rhino curls its lip back to better smell the scents in the air.

Bird Buddies

Rhinos can't see very well. So it's a good thing they've made friends with the sharp-eyed oxpecker. These birds sit perched on the rhino's back while it grazes. The oxpeckers aren't just along for the ride, though. They eat the ticks and other **parasites** that live on the rhino's skin. Sometimes the little birds even enter the big beast's ears and nostrils to reach especially tasty morsels!

In return for the free meal, oxpeckers act as the rhino's alarm system. If the birds sense danger, they'll alert the rhinoceros with loud squawks. This kind of relationship, in which both animals help each other out, is called **symbiosis**.

The oxpecker isn't the rhino's only bird buddy. Larger white birds called cattle egrets follow rhinos around. With every step, the rhino's big feet disturb insects and small animals. That makes it easy for the egret to spot a snack.

▶ Oxpeckers are also called tickbirds, after one of their favorite foods.

CHAPTER 3

Growing Up Rhino

A group of rhinos will happily share a mudhole. But most of the time, rhinos are **solitary** animals. Other than white rhinos, which are a little more social, most species spend almost their entire lives alone.

Dominant bulls are the strongest, highest-ranked male rhinos in an area. They spend most of their time guarding their territories. Sometimes a bull must sneak across another's territory to get to a water source. If he's caught, it can mean trouble. Male rhinos fight to the death to defend their space.

Female rhinos, called cows, are not territorial. They move through areas that often include several males' territories. Sometimes females and their young form groups of a dozen or so. A group of rhinos is called a crash. That's a good name for a bunch of animals big enough to knock over anything in their way!

▶ Rhinos may share a watering hole when they are thirsty.

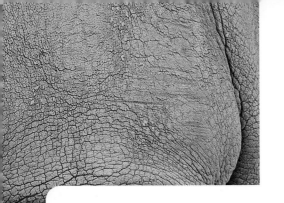

Fast Fact
World Rhino Day
is celebrated on
September 22.

Big Babies

When a female rhino is ready to mate, she walks into a male's territory. As the bull comes over to the cow, he makes noises that sound like hiccups. Then they mate.

The female is pregnant for about 15 months. A rhino baby is called a calf. It weighs between 55 and 100 lb. (24.9 and 45.4 kg) at birth. At first the baby is weak. But within minutes it's strong enough to start walking.

Baby rhinos grow fast on a diet of mother's milk. They can drink as much as 6.6 gal. (25 l) every day! After about a week, they start nibbling on plants. But they keep **nursing** until they're 12 to 18 months old. Rhino mothers and their babies have close bonds.

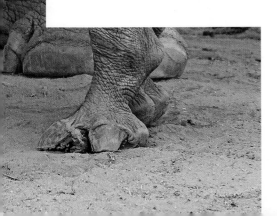

◀ Rhino calves are wobbly for a few days while they learn to walk.

Ready to Go Solo

A three-year old human can't survive without its parents. But by the time a rhino calf is three years old, it is fully grown and ready to take care of itself. Nevertheless, it is not ready to leave its mother just yet. The pair usually live together until the mother rhino is ready to give birth to another calf. That usually happens by the time the first calf is five years old.

That is also the age at which young female rhinos are ready to have calves of their own. Male rhinos, on the other hand, usually don't mate until they are about 10 or 12 years old. That's because they need to have their own territory first. It takes them years to learn the fighting skills they need to claim their own areas.

In the wild, rhinos can live from 18 to 33 years. In zoos, where they are protected from disease and have plenty to eat, they may live as long as 50 years.

◀ This baby black rhino hasn't grown a horn yet.

Ancient Animals

Rhinos look like creatures from an ancient time. And they are! These animals and their ancestors have lumbered across Earth for 55 million years.

When rhinos first appeared, dense forests covered much of the planet. Over time the weather changed. Grasslands grew where forests had been, and rhinos thrived in the new habitat. Species of all shapes and sizes spread across the globe.

One early type of rhino, called *Paraceratherium*, lived about 34 million to 23 million years ago. They looked very different from rhinos today. They didn't have any horns at all, and they were gigantic. Scientists believe some *Paraceratherium* were the largest land animals that have ever lived. They were 16.4 ft. (5 m) tall at the shoulder and weighed more than two school buses!

▶ **This is the skeleton of an extinct woolly rhino that lived more than 10,000 years ago.**

Rhinos Through Time

Another ancient rhino was *Elasmotherium sibiricum*. Its nickname is the "Siberian Unicorn." This rhino emerged about 2.6 million years ago. At 9 ft. (2.7 m) tall, it was no match for *Paraceratherium*. But it had an enormous, thick horn that grew out of the middle of its head. Scientists think its horn may have been longer than 3 ft. (0.9 m)!

About 2.5 million years ago, temperatures on Earth dropped. Snow fell and ice crept across the planet. In response to these chilly temperatures, rhinos **evolved** with thick furry coats. These woolly rhinos lived throughout Europe and Asia. Their frozen remains have been discovered in Siberia, a region in Russia.

Early humans and woolly rhinos lived side by side. Cave paintings made by ancient artists about 30,000 years ago show these animals alongside horses, lions, and mammoths. Prehistoric humans may have hunted woolly rhinos until they went **extinct** just 10,000 years ago. Today history is repeating itself. Humans have once again put many rhinos at risk of disappearing.

◀ Close to 100 rhino species have existed at one time or another.

Curious Cousins

You might guess that the rhino's closest cousin is a hippopotamus. But it is actually a horse!

Rhinoceroses belong to the group of large, plant-eating mammals called perissodactyls. This group also includes horses, zebras, donkeys, and tapirs. Tapirs are piglike animals that live in South and Central America and parts of Asia. This seems like an odd assortment of animals. And it is! The one thing they all have in common is an odd number of toes. Horses, zebras, and donkeys have one toe; rhinos have three. Tapirs have four toes on their front feet—but only three on their back feet.

In 2014, a team of scientists dug up the **fossils** of an ancient rhino relative. It was called *Cambaytherium thewissi*. Experts think it was a chubby creature that weighed between 45 and 75 lb. (20.4 and 34 kg). It walked the Earth about 54.5 million years ago on four or five fingerlike toes. Scientists think that relatives of this strange animal later became modern horses, tapirs, and rhinos.

▶ Which of these animals do *you* think looks most like its cousin the rhino?

Horse

A horse's one "toe" is actually its hoof.

Zebra

Zebras live alongside white and black rhinos in Africa.

Cambaytherium thewissi

Scientists discovered fossils of this ancient rhino relative in Gujarat, India.

Tapir

Like their rhino cousins, tapirs are good swimmers.

CHAPTER 5

Rhinos at Risk

Rhinos need a lot of room to roam.

As the human population grows, forests and grasslands are cut down to make farms. But the biggest threat rhinos face comes from **poaching**.

Humans have prized rhino horns for centuries. In the Middle East, horns are carved into dagger handles. Some people believe that rhino horns have healing powers. They are ground up and sold as medicine. In Asia, a single rhino horn can be sold for as much as $300,000.

Scientists have found no evidence that horns can heal. Rhino hunting has been outlawed, and selling rhino horns is illegal. But every day, poachers break the law and kill these endangered animals. In the last decade, more than 7,000 rhinos have been lost to poaching in Africa alone. By the early 1990s, many rhino species had been almost wiped out. People all over the world began to work to save the remaining rhinos from becoming extinct.

▶ A man in Africa shaves a rhino horn to make traditional medicine.

Fighting for Survival

Protecting rhinos is a big challenge. Conservationists constantly have to find new strategies to stop poachers.

In 2011, African conservationists launched a plan to help black rhinos. They wanted to move them from an area where poaching was common to a safer place. Long journeys by truck can be stressful for animals. So the team came up with a better way. They strapped 19 of the 2,200-lb.(998-kg) rhinos upside down under helicopters! Then they flew them 930 mi. (1,496.7 km) to their new location. Blindfolds helped keep the animals calm on their topsy-turvy journey. After a 10-minute flight, the rhinos landed safely in their new home.

Some of these efforts have been a success. Africa's rhino population is growing. The same is true in India and Nepal. But there is still a lot of work left to do. There are only about 29,000 rhinos left in the wild today. We must all keep fighting to prevent the disappearance of these extradordinary animals from our planet.

◄ This rhino will be microchipped so that scientists can track it.

Rhinoceros Family Tree

Rhinoceroses belong to the order Perissodactyla, also known as odd-toed ungulates. All the animals in this order are mammals characterized by an odd number of toes. They all share a common ancestor that lived about 55 million years ago. This diagram shows how rhinos are related to other perissodactyls, such as tapirs, horses, camels, giraffes, pigs, and deer. The closer together two animals are on the tree, the more similar they are.

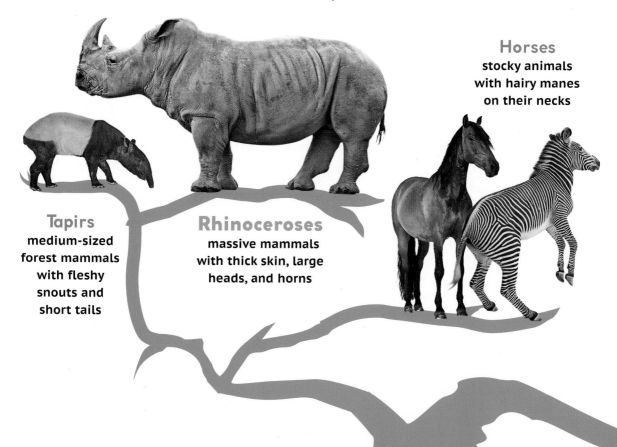

Horses
stocky animals with hairy manes on their necks

Tapirs
medium-sized forest mammals with fleshy snouts and short tails

Rhinoceroses
massive mammals with thick skin, large heads, and horns

Ancestor of all Perissodactyls

Note: Animal photos are not to scale.

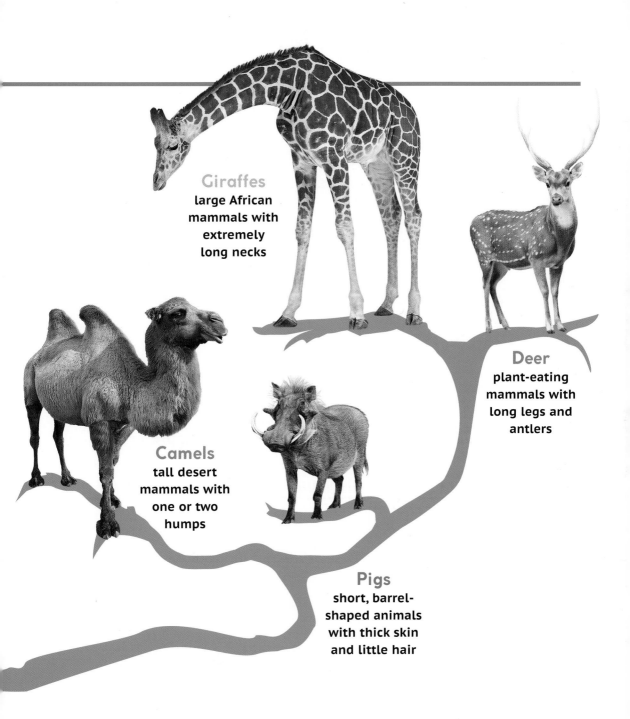

Giraffes
large African mammals with extremely long necks

Deer
plant-eating mammals with long legs and antlers

Camels
tall desert mammals with one or two humps

Pigs
short, barrel-shaped animals with thick skin and little hair

Words to Know

A .... **ancestors** *(ANN-ses-turz)* family members who lived long ago

C .... **conservationists** *(kahn-sur-VAY-shun-ists)* people who protect valuable things, especially forests, wildlife, or natural resources

D .... **dominant** *(DAH-muh-nuhnt)* most influential or powerful

E .... **endangered** *(en-DAYN-juhrd)* a plant or animal that is in danger of becoming extinct, usually because of human activity

evolved *(i-VAHLVD)* changed slowly and naturally over time

extinct *(ik-STINGKT)* no longer found alive

F .... **fossils** *(FAH-suhls)* bones, shells, or other traces of an animal or plant from millions of years ago, preserved as rock

H .... **habitats** *(HAB-i-tats)* the places where an animal or plant is usually found

herbivores *(HUR-buh-vors)* animals that eat only plants

I .... **infrasonic** *(in-fruh-SAH-nik)* a sound too low for the human ear to hear

K .... **keratin** *(KER-uh-tin)* a substance that makes up feathers, nails, hooves, hair, and horns

M .... **mammals** *(MAM-uhls)* warm-blooded animals that have hair or fur and usually give birth to live babies; female mammals produce milk to feed their young

N .... **nursing** *(NURS-ing)* drinking milk from a breast

P .... **parasites** *(PAR-uh-sites)* animals or plants that live on or inside another animal or plant

poaching *(POHCH-ing)* hunting or fishing illegally on someone else's property

population *(pahp-yuh-LAY-shuhn)* all members of a species living in a certain place

predators *(PRED-uh-tuhrs)* animals that live by hunting other animals for food

prehensile *(pree-HEN-suhl)* adapted for seizing or grasping, especially by wrapping around

prey *(PRAY)* an animal that is hunted by another animal for food

S .... **savanna** *(suh-VAN-uh)* a flat, grassy plain with few or no trees

solitary *(SAH-li-ter-ee)* not requiring or without the companionship of others

species *(SPEE-sheez)* one of the groups into which animals and plants are divided; members of the same species can mate and have offspring

symbiosis *(sim-bee-OH-sis)* a close relationship between two different kinds of living things, usually to the advantage of both

T .... **territory** *(TER-i-tor-ee)* an area that an animal or a group of animals uses and defends

V .... **vocalize** *(VOH-kuh-lize)* to make sounds to communicate

W .... **wallowing** *(WAH-loh-ing)* rolling around in mud or water

Find Out More

BOOKS

- Hamilton, Garry. *Rhino Rescue: Changing the Future for Endangered Wildlife*. New York: Firefly Books, 2006.
- Kelly, Mina. *The Most Amazing Fact Book for Kids About Rhinos*. Kid's U: 2016.
- Meeker, Clare Hodgson. *National Geographic Kids Chapters: Rhino Rescue: And More True Stories of Saving Animals*. Washington, D.C.: National Geographic Children's Books, 2016.

WEB PAGES

- www.worldwildlife.org/species/rhino

  Information about conservation efforts from the World Wildlife Fund.
- http://kids.sandiegozoo.org/animals/rhinoceros

  Kid-friendly facts and photos about the different rhino species from the San Diego Zoo.
- www.savetherhino.org/rhino_info/species_of_rhino

  Learn about rhinoceroses and what you can do to help them.

Facts for Now

Visit this Scholastic Web site for more information on rhinoceroses:
www.factsfornow.scholastic.com Enter the keyword **Rhinoceroses**

Index

Index *(continued)*

About the Author

Stephanie Warren Drimmer writes books and magazine stories for kids. She covers all topics weird and wonderful, but especially loves adorable animals and strange planets. Stephanie studied science journalism at New York University and lives in Los Angeles, California.